Edward Doubleday Harris

A Copy of the Old Epitaphs in the Burying Ground of

Block-Island, R I

Edward Doubleday Harris

A Copy of the Old Epitaphs in the Burying Ground of Block-Island, R I

ISBN/EAN: 9783337192150

Printed in Europe, USA, Canada, Australia, Japan

Cover: Foto ©ninafisch / pixelio.de

More available books at **www.hansebooks.com**

· A · COPY · OF ·

· THE · OLD · EPITAPHS ·

· IN · THE · BURYING · GROUND ·

OF

· BLOCK-ISLAND ·
· R · I ·

·BY · EDW · DOUBLEDAY · HARRIS·
· MEMBER · OF · THE · MASS · HISTORICAL · SOCIETY ·

· CAMBRIDGE · 1883 ·
· PRESS · OF · JOHN · WILSON · AND · SON ·

TO

MY LIFE-LONG AND HONORED FRIEND,

JOHN LANGDON SIBLEY,

LIBRARIAN EMERITUS OF HARVARD COLLEGE,

THIS MEMORY OF A SUMMER'S VACATION

IS INSCRIBED.

BLOCK ISLAND, named for the Dutch explorer, Adrian Block, is in latitude 41° 08' North, and longitude 71° 33' West. It is distant southwest from Newport about thirty miles, and north of east from Montauk, the easterly end of Long Island, about eighteen miles.

It was first described in the year 1524 by the French navigator, Verrazzano. In 1614 it was visited by Block, who gave it its present name. In 1636 the Boston trader, John Oldham, while at anchor in its harbor, was killed by the Indians. Colonel John Endicott was soon afterwards sent by the General Court of Massachusetts to punish the offenders. He landed upon the Island and thoroughly accomplished his object. In 1658 the Island was granted to Gov. Endicott, Deputy Governor Richard Bellingham, Major General Daniel Dennison and Major William Hathorne, who in turn sold it in 1660 to Doctor John Alcock of Roxbury and his associates.

The year 1662 witnessed the first white settlement of the Island by a company from Boston and Taunton.

The old Cemetery from which the inscriptions on the following pages were taken is situated on the westerly side of a hill overlooking the Great Salt Pond. Many of its graves are marked simply by round field stones gathered from the neighborhood.

Most of the older inscribed stones are of slate, ornamented with the conventional winged skull and scroll borders, precisely like many in the sea-board towns of the mainland. These stones were undoubtedly imported from England already ornamented, and were lettered by a skilled hand in this country. A few of the stones are from the sandstone quarries of Connecticut, and these are generally devoid of ornamentation.

It is believed that exact copies of the inscriptions of all the stones antedating 1800 will be found in these pages.

EDWARD DOUBLEDAY HARRIS.

Brooklyn, N. Y., April, 1883.

·BLOCK-ISLAND · EPITAPHS·

[*Thick sandstone without ornamentation.*]

HEARE LIETH

THE BODY OF M

MARGRET GVTRY

AGED 64 YERS WHO

DEPARTED   THIS

LIFE APRIL 5 1687

Robert Guthrig was Town Clerk in 1675, and probably the same Mr. Robart Guttereg, or Guttrig, was freeman of the colony in 1684, and died in 1692. The surname is a corruption of Goodrich, a family numerous in Connecticut at that time.

[*Horizontal sandstone slab.*]

HERE LYES IN

TVRRED ŦE BODY

OF MR IÆMES SÆNDS

SENIOVR ADED 73

YEÆRS DEPÆRTED

THIS LIFE MÆRCH

THE 13 1695

James Sands, with wife Sarah, though not in the first company, was of the Island early enough to participate in first division of lands. He was a freeman in 1655, and was Representative in 1678, 1680, and 1690. He had sons, John, James, and Samuel, who settled at Cowneck, L. I., Edward, and Job, and daughters, Sarah (who married Nathaniel Niles) and Mercy (who married Joshua Raymond). His wife Sarah died before July 6, 1702.

Captain John Sands and James Sands, Jr., were freemen of the Island in 1684.

[Horizontal sandstone slab.]

HERE   LYETH   INTERRED

THE BODY OF CAPT^N

EDWARD SANDS WHO

DEPARTED THIS LIFE JVNE

Y^e 14 1708 IN Y^e [illeg.]

YEARE OF HIS AGE

Edward Sands was the youngest son of James, the first settler. The figures denoting the age are illegible on the gravestone. Livermore deciphers them as 43. He was made freeman in 1696; left at his decease a wife and daughter Sarah, but probably no other children.

[*Slate-stone.*]

Here Lieth y^e

Body of Thomas

Dickens who died

Sep^t ye 4th 1718

Aged 50 Years.

His wife Sarah died 1733.
Nathaniel Dickens was freeman of Providence in 1655.

[*Slate-stone.*]

Here lyeth
William Son
of Nathanael
Dun and of
Elizabeth his
wife dyed May
ye 16th 1721
aged 6 years

[*Slate-stone.*]

Here Lieth y^e

Body of Sarah

ye Wife of Thomas

Dickens who

died April ye 3^d

1733 aged 59

Years.

[*Slate-stone.*]

Here lieth y^e

Body of Truſtrum

Dodge died

Aug^{ſt} 18th 1733

In ye 87th year

of his age.

Probably the son of the member of the first company of the same name, whose name is in the list of freemen with his father's in 1678, designated respectively as Senior and Junior. The grave of the elder man is not marked.

[*Slate-stone.*]

Here lieth ye Body

of Nathaniel Mott

died Sept^m ye 14th

1733 In ye 26th

year of his age.

Nathaniel and John Mott were freemen in 1678, the former being Town Recorder or Clerk in 1695, and holding the office for many years. He was Representative to the General Court, also, in 1710.

Edward Mott was Constable in 1700.

[*Slate-stone.*]

Here lieth ye Body
of Captn Thomas
Rathbun died Decem^r
ye 26th 1733 Aged
76 Years.

Thomas Rathbone, a freeman of 1678, was probably a son of John. He was Representative in 1700, and for several years afterwards.

[*Slate-stone.*]

In Memory of

Nathaniel Dunn

died Febr^y y^c 28th

1735 Aged

64 Years.

The name does not occur in the early lists of settlers or freemen.

Here lieth

James ye Son of

Jeremiah & Mary

Sheffield died

Septr ye 8th 1736

Aged 2 Years

& 6 M^o.

[*Slate-stone.*]

Here

Lies ye Body

of Darkis ye widow of

Truſtrum Dodge who

Died Feb^{ry} ye 18

1737 in ye 74th

year of her Age

[Horizontal slate-stone slab.]

THIS MONUMENT
Is erected to the Memory
of SIMON RAY Efquire
One of the original Proprietors
of this Ifland
He was largely concerned
In setling the Townfhip
And was one of the chief Magiftrates
and such was his Benevolence
That besides the care which he took
Of their civil Interefts
He frequently inftructed them
In the more important Concerns
Of our Holy Religion
He was deprived of his Eyefight many Years
Cheerfully fubmitting to the will of God
His Life being in this trying Inftance
As in all others
A Lovely Example of Chriftian Virtue
He died on the 17th of March 1737
In the 102nd Year of his Age.

Simon Ray, Senior, was the son of Simon of Braintree, Mass., who died
there 30 Sept., 1641. He was one of the original proprietors of Block Island,
and was in the Taunton company that arrived there in 1661. In 1676 he was
Deputy Warden and afterward Warden of the Island, was a freeman in 1664,
and for many years represented the colony in the General Assembly.

He married Mary, daughter of Nathaniel Thomas of Marshfield, Mass., and
had issue: Mary, b. May 19, 1667; Dorothy, b. Oct. 16, 1669; Simon, b.
April 9, 1672; Sibel, b. March 19, 1675.

In Memory of

Sarah y^c Wife

of Henry Willis

died Sep^t y^c 8

1738 Aged

49 Years.

[*Slate-stone.*]

Here lieth ye Body
of William ye Son
of Ebenezer &
Ann Dodge died
Jany. ye 26 1739
Aged 3 Yrs. 3
M^o & 16 Days.

Trustam or Trustarum Dodge (sometimes spelled Daudg
or Daug in the old records) was one of the first company from
Taunton in 1661, was a town officer in 1676, had been admitted freeman in 1664, was living in 1684, and is thought to
have been the ancestor of the after generations of Dodges
on the Island. John and William Dodge, and a Trustarum,
perhaps sons of the first settler, were freemen in 1678.

[Horizontal slab of slate-stone.]

IN MEMORY OF

Rebecca $\overset{e}{y}$ Wife of

Mr Ackrus Tofh died

April $\overset{e}{y}$ 15th 1739 In $\overset{e}{y}$

44th year of her age.

[*Horizontal slab of slate-stone.*]

IN MEMORY OF

Mʳ. Ackurs Tofh died

June ẙ 21ᶠᵗ 1739 In ẙ

54ᵗʰ year of his age.

William Tosh was a passenger in the ship that carried the first company of settlers from Taunton in 1661. He was made freeman in 1664, constable in 1676, and died in 1685; probably the father of Ackurs.

Daniel Tosh, probably a brother of William, was freeman in 1684. Both seem to have escaped the notice of Savage.

[*Slate-stone.*]

In Memory of

Capt Thomas

Mitchel Junr died

March y̆^e 29th 1741

in ye 59th year of

of his age.

Capt. Thomas Mitchell, Jr., was probably the son of the Thomas whose name was enrolled among the Freemen in 1678, and who is named in Niles's account of the Indian and French Wars in 1689, Mass. Hist. Coll., 3d Series, Vol. VI.

[*Slate-stone.*]

In Memory of
Elizabeth ye Wife
of Nathaniel Dunn
died May ye 19th
1741 Aged
69 Years.

[*Slate-stone.*]

In Memory of

Patience y^e

Wife of Samuel

Rathbun died

Aug^{ft} ye 3^d 1747.

[*Slate-stone.*]

.

Sarah   Daughter

of Edward &

Mary   Ball

died   Decem^r

ye 23rd 1747

Aged I Year

& I Month

An Edward Ball was enrolled in the Freeman list as early as 1678.   John and Peter Ball were freemen in 1709.

[*Slate-stone.*]

In Memory of
Joſhua y^e Son of
Mark & Lydia
Dodge died Jan^y
y^e 1 1747/8 Aged
1 Year & 2 Months

[*Slate-stone.*]

Dorothy y^e

Daughter

of Nathanael

& Ann Lock

died Novr 3^d

1749 Aged 8 M^o

[*Slate-stone.*]

In Memory of
Amous $\overset{e}{y}$ Son
of Samuel & Pru
dence Champlin
died Febr^y y^e 11th
1749/50 in y^e 11th
year of his age

[*Slate-stone.*]

Dorothy y^e

2^d Daughter

of Nathanael

& Ann Lock

died Novr 16th

1750 Aged

1 Year 1 M^o &

6 Days

In Memory of

Prudence y^e Wife

of Samuel Champlin

died Janr^y y^e

28th 1750/1 in y^e

34th year of her age

[*Slate-stone.*]

Abraham Son
of Joſeph &
Neomy Mitchell
died Novr 9th
1751 Aged 1 Year
1 M^o & 27 Days

[*Slate-stone.*]

Elizabeth y^e

Daughter of

Thomas & Judi

th Hubbart

died Novr y^e

13 1751 Aged

3 Years 8 M^o

& 17 Days

Thomas Hubbard was of Boston, and his wife Judith was the eldest daughter of Capt. Simon Ray.

[*Slate-stone.*]

In Memory

of John Mott

who died Aug^{ft} 2 5th

1753 in ye 53^{d}

Year of his Age

John Mott was admitted freeman in 1721.

[*Horizontal slate-stone slab.*]

Beneath THIS STONE
Are depofited the Remains
of SIMON RAY Efquire
Who for many Years
Was one of the chief Magistrates of this Town
He filled the moft important Offices
With honor to Himfelf
And Advantage to his Country.
To fupprefs Vice and promote Virtue
was the fixed Aim of his private Life
And public Authority
He was a Lover of Learning
Justice and Benevolence
A Friend to his Country and ever attentive
to the Interefts of this Ifland
He was a fincere Believer in our Saviour
And by a faithful Obedience to his Precepts
Truly adorned the Chriftian profefsion
He died on the 9th March 1755
In the 85th Year of his Age.

Simon Ray was born 9 April, 1672, on the Island, the only son of Simon, the first settler, by wife Mary. He had issue: Judith, b. Oct. 4, 1726, married Thomas Hubbard; Anna, b. Sept. 27, 1728, married Samuel Ward, afterward Governor of Rhode Island; Catharine, b. July 10, 1731, married William Greene, also a Governor of Rhode Island; Phebe, b. Sept. 10, 1733, married John Littlefield.

[*Slate-stone.*]

In Memory of

Ann ye Wife of

Nathanael Lock

who died May

ye 11th A.D. 1755

[*Slate-stone.*]

In Memory of
Ann Daughter of
Nehemiah & Mary
Dodge who died
July ye 29 1755
Aged 39 Years

[*Sandstone.*]

Here Lẙth The Body of
Willm Greffeth Borne Sep.^r
12th 1715 Drowned at Block
Island October 19th 1755
Aged 40 Years

[*Slate-stone.*]

Matthia Son

of William &

Katharine Rock

died Novr ye 4th

1755   Aged

16 Years.

[*Slate-stone.*]

In Memory of

Samuel Rathbun

who died Janr^y 24th

1757 in ye 85th

Year of his Age.

John Rathbone was one of the first company from Taunton in 1661, and one of the first landholders. The list of freemen of 1678 includes the names of John, Senior and Junior, Thomas, and William. The Samuel above was probably a grandson of the elder John, and was born 3 Aug., 1672. His wife, Patience, died 3 Aug., 1747.

[*Slate-stone.*]

In Memory of
Abigail ye Wife of
Jonathan Mitchell
who died April 9th
A.D. 1757 in y^e
60th Year of
her Age.

Jonathan Mitchell was admitted freeman in 1728.

James Mitchell is said by Livermore to have been freeman in 1683. Thomas Mitchell was admitted in 1678, and was probably the father of the Lieutenant and Captain of the same name but of later date, and the ancestor of the Block Island families.

[*Slate-stone.*]

Samuel George

Son of Joſeph &

Neomy Mitchell

died Novr 10th

1759 Aged 3

Years 11 M^o 5

Days

[*Slate-stone.*]

IN MEMORY of
Alice the Wife of
M^r. Carder Hazard
who died Jany ye 1st
1760 in ye 21st Year
of Her Age.

She was a Kind Wife
A Tender Parent
And a worthy Friend.

[*Slate-stone.*]

IN MEMORY OF

Hannah ye Wife of

Edward Sands E/q^r.

who died Janr^y. 18th

A.D. 1760 in the

52^d Year of her Age.

[*Slate-stone.*]

IN MEMORY of

MERCY wife of M.ʳ

CALEB LITTLEFIELD

who died April yᵉ 3ᵈ A.D.

1761 in yᵉ 66ᵗʰ Year of

her Age.

Caleb Littlefield was made freeman in 1721. The name, although common on the Island in later years, did not occur until that date.

[Slate-stone.]

IN MEMORY of
PHEBE yᵉ youngeſt Daughter
of SIMON RAY Eſqʳ. & Wife
of JOHN LITTLEFIELD
Eſqʳ. was born 27ᵗʰ Sepᵗ.
1733 & died April yᵉ 30ᵗʰ
1761.

[*Slate-stone.*]

IN MEMORY of
Elizabeth the Wife
of M^r. John Sands
who died Aug^{ft} 31^{ft}
A.D. 1765 in ye 19th .
Year of her Age

Stop Reader spend a mournful tear
Upon the Duft that slumbers Here
And while you Read the state of me
Think on the Glafs that runs for thee.

[*Slate-stone.*]

In Memory
of Abigail
Wife of
Samuel Dunn
who died
July 17th 1771
in the 29th
Year of
her Age.

[*Slate-stone.*]

Sacred
to the Memory of
EDWARD SANDS Efq.
who died October 21^{ft} 1778
Aged 66 Years
Having sustained several
Offices of public Trust
and discharged the
relative Duties of Life
with Credit to his Country
and Honour to himself

[*Slate-stone.*]

In Memory
of
SIMON RAY LITTLEFIELD
Eſq.^{r}

who departed this Life

March 31^{ſt} 1780

in the 29th Year of his

Age.

[*Sandstone.*]

This Stone is Erected
by the Affectionate
and Afflicted parents
of *Samuel Gruman* 2^{d}
of Norwalk in Connec
ticut who was drowned
June 14th 1791 near
Crab-Meadow Long
Ifland in the 27th year
of his age

[*Slate-stone.*]

In Memory of

Hannah   wife of M^r.

JAMES ROSE

who departed this Life

december 1st 1791 in the

60th year of her Age

She was a kind wife, a tender
Parent and beloved by all her
A^{c}quaintance.

[*Slate-stone.*]

In Memory of

Samuel Beckwith Mitchell

Son of Dickens & Sarah

Mitchell, died June 21st 1794

in the 8th year of his Age.

This lovely youth to death bowed
down
While friend and parents round him
mourn.

[*Brown-stone.*]

In MEMORY of
Mrs. MARY BRIGGS
the *Virtuous* Confort of
Mr. NATHANIEL BRIGGS
fhe died March 7th 1795
aged 25 years

A Lady highly refpected for
her domeftic virtues and for
her exemplary piety — but !
How lov'd how valued once avails thee not
To whom related or by whom begot.

[*Slate-stone.*]

In Memory of

JOHN LITTLEFIELD

Efq.ᵣ

who died June 13ᵗʰ 1796

aged 79 years 3 M⁰ & 13 days.

John Littlefield was a son of Caleb and Mercy of Block Island. He was admitted freeman in 1738, was Representative in 1747, and for many following years.

[*Brown-stone.*]

In Memory of
Mr. Edward Ball
who died June 17th 1796
in the 70th year of his age
A kind huſband tender Father
affectionate friend and well
beloved by all his acquaintance

As you paſs by pray caſt an eye
As you are now ſo once was I
As I am now ſo muſt you be
Prepare for death and follow me.

One Edward Ball was on the freeman list of 1684, but he
was probably a resident as early as 1678. He is supposed to
have been the ancestor of all the later individuals of the name
on the island.

[Brown-stone.]

In memory of
Mr. Daniel Mott
who departed
this life June 14th
1798 in the 57th
year of his age

*He was a kind and loving
husband and tender
parent.*

[*Slate-stone.*]

In memory of

Mr TORMETT ROSE,

who died June 1st

1803,

in the 73^d year

of his age.

The original settler spelled his name Thormut or Tormot. He was one of the first company from Taunton in 1661, and was assigned land there in the first division. He was early a Town Officer, was made freeman in 1664, and was living certainly as late as 1684. The same Christian name has been perpetuated in the family under various spellings, until, according to Livermore, it has assumed the form of *Thomas*.

William Rose was the captain of the vessel that brought the first company to the island, but it does not appear that he remained.

[*Slate-stone.*]

In

Memory of

Janette Sherry

Daughter of

Burton & Huldey Briggs

who died May 2nd 1804

aged 2 month & 9 days

[*Slate-stone.*]

SACRED

to

the Memory

of

PHEBE

amiable confort of

Mr. TREADWELL SANDS

who died

March 27th A. D. 1805

in the 39th year of

her age.

INDEXES.

INDEX OF EPITAPHS.

GENERAL INDEX.